Isaac Drandić is an award-winning theatre-maker and one of Australia's leading voices in contemporary First Nations performance. A Noongar man from the south-west of Western Australia, he is nationally recognised for his work as a director, dramaturg, actor and playwright, and for his leadership in the development of new First Nations works across the country. He currently serves as Head of First Nations Theatre at Queensland Theatre, following significant appointments as Associate Artistic Director/Resident Dramaturg at Queensland Theatre, Resident Artist at Playwriting Australia, and Associate Director at ILBIJERRI Theatre Company.

Isaac's directing and dramaturgy credits span mainstage companies and major festivals, including *Dear Son* (Queensland Theatre/State Theatre Company South Australia), *Dear Brother* (Queensland Theatre), *37* (Queensland Theatre/Melbourne Theatre Company), *The Visitors* (Victorian Opera), *The Season* and *Hide the Dog* (Performing Lines), *At What Cost?* and *Coranderrk* (Belvoir), *City of Gold* (Queensland Theatre/Griffin Theatre Company), *Blood on the Dance Floor* (ILBIJERRI), *Bigger and Blacker*, *From Darkness* (La Boite), *From Campfire to Stage Light* (JUTE), and co-directing Archie Roach's acclaimed concert work *Into the Bloodstream*. As a playwright, Isaac's plays for children have toured extensively to remote communities including Pormpuraaw, Mornington Island, Camooweal and Normanton, reaching more than 20,000 young people. Isaac's accolades include multiple Green Room Awards, including Best Direction and Best Production for *The Season*, and Matilda Awards for Best Direction and Best Production for *37*. He remains dedicated to culturally informed storytelling, community engagement, and the mentorship of emerging First Nations writers and creatives, bringing powerful, place-rooted stories to stages and communities across Australia.

JOHN HARVEY is a playwright and multidisciplinary artist whose work spans theatre, film and installation and is of Saibai Island (Torres Strait) and English descent.

His theatre writing includes: *The Return* (Malthouse Theatre), winner of the 2023 Victorian Premier's Literary Award for Drama; *Dear Son* (Queensland Theatre, State Theatre Company of South Australia); *Heart is a Wasteland* (Malthouse Theatre, ILBIJERRI Theatre, Yirra Yaakin Theatre); and international co-production *Black Ties* (ILBIJERRI Theatre / Tē Rehia) presented at Asia TOPA, Sydney, Auckland Festivals). He is the inaugural recipient of the First Nations Writers Residency (FNAWN, AAA) in New York and Boston and has held writer residencies at Malthouse Theatre and Footscray Arts. He directed *A Little Piece of Heaven* (Orana Arts) for the Yirramboi Arts Festival. His screen directing credits include: the award-winning documentaries *Still We Rise* (ABC), recipient of the 2023 AIDC and ADG Best Documentary Awards, and *Off Country* (NITV), winner of the 2022 ADG Award for Best Documentary. His acclaimed short film *Katele (Mudskipper)* won Best Australian Short Film at Flickerfest and MIFF. He produced *Spear,* premiering at Toronto International Film Festival, *Sand* from *The Turning* (Biennale) and ABC series *The Warriors.*

John's collaboration with Walter Waia, *The Heart of the Universe*, is a major multi-channel video and sound installation for the 2026 Biennale of Sydney, and his work *Canopy* is part of the permanent installation for ACMI, later realised as public mural for Melbourne Metro. A 2023 Sidney Myer Creative Fellow, he is the Creative Director of Brown Cabs and board member of Bangarra Dance Theatre.

THOMAS MAYO is an Aboriginal and Torres Strait Islander man and a father of five who was born and raised on Larrakia Country in Darwin. He is an award-winning author of seven books and is the Assistant National Secretary of the Maritime Union of Australia. He serves as a board member for the Indigenous Literacy Foundation among numerous other board positions in his trade union work.

Thomas was entrusted with the Uluru Statement from the Heart after participating in the Uluru National Constitutional Convention in 2017, taking it around Australia to build the campaign for a constitutionally enshrined Voice and a Makarrata Commission. He was a prominent leader in the referendum campaign for a Voice in 2023 and continues to advocate for justice and recognition for Indigenous peoples.

Dear Son

Adapted by **ISAAC DRANDIĆ**
and **JOHN HARVEY**

Based on the book
by **THOMAS MAYO**

Letters and reflections from
First Nations fathers and sons

CURRENCY PRESS
The performing arts publisher

CURRENCY PLAYS

First published in 2026
by Currency Press Pty Ltd,
Gadigal Land, Suite 310, 46–56 Kippax Street, Surry Hills, NSW 2010, Australia
enquiries@currency.com.au
www.currency.com.au

Typeset by Brighton Gray for Currency Press.
Printed by Fineline Print + Copy Services, Revesby, NSW.
Cover shows Aaron Pedersen; photo by David Kelly.
Cover design by Katherine Zhang for Currency Press.

Currency Press acknowledges the Traditional Owners of the Country on which we live and work. We pay our respects to all Aboriginal and Torres Strait Islander Elders, past and present.

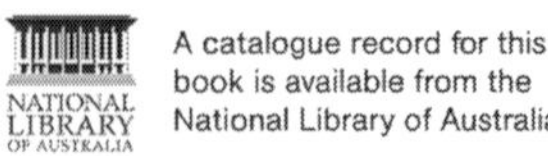

Contents

Aaron Pedersen in Queensland Theatre's production of Dear Son, *2025*
(Photo © David Kelly/Copyright Agency, 2025)

Director's Note

Writing Between Generations—Bloodlines on Stage

In many First Nations cultures, knowledge is passed not just through speech, but through story, silence, and gesture. But sometimes, when the words are too heavy to say out loud, we turn to paper. To write is not only to remember—it is to resist, to reclaim, and to reach across generations.

This story holds a letter that is not yet spoken. A letter from a son to his father. From a father to his son. A radical act of love written in a time of struggle, seeking not to fix what's broken but to understand where the break began.

To write in this way—from a Black man to his old man, and to his boy—is to thread truth through bloodlines. It is to say: *I see you. I come from you. I fight for you.*

This is not just a letter. It is a song without music. A protest without shouting. A story that moves between ring and fire, between pride and pain.

But this production is more than a play—it is a gathering of story, spirit, and memory. At its heart is a conversation between a father and a son. But that conversation does not live only on the page or the stage. It lives in the hearts and histories of the men telling it.

Each actor in the original production is, in their own life, a father, a son, or both. They carry with them not just a script, but real memories of their old men, their boys, their uncles and pops. They walk into this work with the weight of lived experience—the kind of experience that can't be taught in drama school, only lived and felt.

To perform this story—one that cuts so close to the bone—takes courage. Not just artistic courage, but cultural and emotional courage. The men who step onto the stage aim not to pretend, but to reveal. They allow the audience to witness something raw and rarely shared: the complexity of love between Black men. The silence, the shame, the pride, the distance—and the deep, unspoken knowing.

They are not merely playing characters. They are standing in a long line of warriors and workers, of fathers who did their best with what they had, and sons who are trying to do better. This work is an offering. A ceremony. A letter back in time and forward again.

And through their open, honest and raw performances, they remind us: the most radical thing we can do is love our fathers, love our sons, and find new ways to speak the truth between us.

In this space, we invite you to listen not only with your ears, but with your spirit. The words may not be your own, but the ache—the longing to be understood, to be seen—that is something we all carry.

Isaac Drandić

Co-Adaptor's Note

There's a saying—men don't talk.

Or rather, we don't 'talk talk'.

We talk about footy, cars, politics.

Anything but what's really going on inside.'

And that's okay, until you think that for all our silence, men take up a lot of space in this world. We lead companies. We lead communities. We lead countries. And yet, we remain painfully aware of toxic masculinity, violence against women, damage in our communities—even as the statistics refuse to shift.

The door to change has often felt closed or like a wound that won't heal. In these letters of *Dear Son*, thirteen brave Indigenous men invite us into their intimate relationship with their sons and fathers—and ask us to sit with vulnerability, truth and love.

The process of creating this work brought together Indigenous men—actors, director, writers—into a room, drawn together by the book *Dear Son*. But as we began to speak about the letters, something shifted and we began to speak about our own personal lives. Stories we hadn't shared before. Not because we didn't trust each other—we've known each other for years—but because so often, as men, we carry things in silence. The book gave us permission to speak what had long been unspoken.

We felt the power of *Dear Son* immediately. It opened something in us—a space to share emotion, vulnerability and challenges. That's the spirit that shapes this stage adaptation.

Our outer worlds reflect our inner worlds. The world that we are trying to create—safe, kind, connected—begins when we unlock the world within. As Bob Marley's words remind us, echoing in the Cook Haus gatherings and backyard BBQs across our communities: 'Emancipate yourself from mental slavery, none but ourselves can free our mind.' There is no end point, no destination; simply a journey.

We are sons of mothers, who knew our fathers, and brought us into this world, who gave us life, and loved us. Whose soft touch endured even when the world was against them, who put others before themselves. We are fathers of sons and daughters, who look to us to understand what a good man looks like. We have wives, partners and loved ones whose strength and love keeps the home fires burning, so that we can carry this story. We are thankful for all that you are, and all that you do.

We thank the actors, creatives and everyone from the villages of Queensland Theatre and State Theatre Company of South Australia who came together to tell this story. And the financial partners who stand with us to tell this story, we thank you. As co-writers, we're fathers who lived across the road from each other—on the same street, with babies born on the same day. And there we were, wheelie bins in one hand, babies in the other, never imagining how much those little ones and our older ones would shape us in ways we couldn't yet understand.

John Harvey

Dear Son was first produced by Queensland Theatre at the Bille Browne Theatre, Jagera and Turrbal Country, Brisbane, on 28 June 2025 with the following cast and creatives:

Jimi Bani
Waangenga Blanco
Trevor Jamieson
Kirk Page
Aaron Pedersen

Director and Co-Adaptor, Isaac Drandić
Co-Adaptor, John Harvey
Set Designer, Kevin O'Brien
Costume Designer, Delvene Cockatoo-Collins
Lighting Designer, David Walters
Video Designer, Craig Wilkinson
Composer and Sound Designer, Wil Hughes
Choreography and Movement Director, Waangenga Blanco
Associate Lighting Designer, Eben Love
Associate Composer and Sound Designer, Patrick Mau
Assistant Director, Tibian Wyles
Associate Construction and Set Designer, Liam Maza
Vocal Coach, Marcus Oborn
Happiness Consultant, Vinnie Pedersen
Stage Manager, Pip Loth
Assistant Stage Manager, Yanni Dubler

CHARACTERS

MAN 1
MAN 2
MAN 3
MAN 4
MAN 5

STAGING NOTES

At the start of each scene, the respective scene title should be projected onstage. This is to reflect the chapters of the original *Dear Son* anthology, on which the play is based.

PROLOGUE—THE SPOTLIGHT OF SOCIETY

The following play is based on letters from fathers to sons and a couple from sons to fathers.

The projected text fades.

Five MEN *enter the space. They are in the spotlight. The spotlight of society.*

Soundscape—Atmospheric.

Projection—'Father, Son, Brother, Uncle, Husband, Engineer, Builder, Warrior, Leader ... '

And other positive examples of Indigenous men.

Projection—Colonial labels begin to invade the space. The MEN *take off layers of clothing: 'Cannibals, Heathens, Primitive, Savages, Nomads, Flora, Fauna, Blacks, Devil Worshippers ... '*

Soundscape of labels and media vitriol invades the space.

Projection continues—modern labels: 'Criminals, Perpetrators, Molesters, Paedophiles, Rapists, Drunks, Bludgers, Lazy, Stupid, Dumb ... '

Projection continues—racist labels, sound builds: 'Abo, Coon, Boong, Monkey, Darkie, Nigger ... '

The five MEN *respond. Singing out their own clan names.*

MAN 2: …

MAN 3: …

MAN 1: …

MAN 4: …

MAN 5: …

> *The five* MEN *sing out the clan names of the letter-writers from the book.*

MAN 2: Gumbaynggir, Bunjalung

MAN 3: Kulkalgal

MAN 4: Noongar, Yamatji, Gija

MAN 5: Birpai—Thungutti
MAN 2: Gundaji, Wambaya
MAN 3: Arrernte, Luritja
MAN 4: Wiradjuri, Wolgalu, Erubamle
MAN 5: Gundungurra, Ngunawal
MAN 4: Gurindji
MAN 2: Yorta Yorta, Gunaikurnai

Beat.

The MEN *speak the name of the Country the story is being performed on. They have prepared themselves and the space.*

CHORUS: …
CHORUS: With the strength of our ancestors.
MAN 2: We pull the oars of truth …
MAN 1: Against the tides of ignorance and toxic masculinity.
CHORUS: With the strength of our ancestors …
MAN 5: Our words, as bright as the stars on a moonless night.
MAN 4: We offer our children …
MAN 3: Shining points of guidance.
CHORUS: We pull the oars of truth …
MAN 1: Dear Son …
MAN 2: Dear Son.
MAN 3: Dear Son.
MAN 4: Dear Son.
MAN 5: Dear Son.

The MEN *gather their shirts/costumes and place them in compartments onstage. All exit except* MAN 1. MAN 1 *takes a seat.*

The lights dim as …

ACT I—LETTERS OF LONGING

SCENE 1: HE TRIED TO TAKE MY HAND

The Cook Haus—an informal gathering place of this men's group. It's a place where men gather, yarn, and cook. The Cook Haus has been damaged in a storm, the roof and parts strewn on the ground.

MAN 1 *writes.*

MAN 1: Hello Son …
Dear mate …
What am I trying to say?
You are my son … [*Sarcastically*] 'Thanks Dad.'
Shit …

MAN 2, MAN 3, MAN 4, MAN 5 *enter.*

MAN 2: This is going to be brilliant.
MAN 3: You made one of these before?
MAN 2: Yeah of course, brother.
MAN 5: Where do you want this tin?
MAN 2: Bring it over here, we'll get these beams on first.

The MEN *place the side posts of the Cook Haus in first. There are now four posts standing.*

MAN 3: What happened here?
MAN 2: The storm took the roof off.

MAN 2 *notices* MAN 1 *in his own world.*

Which way, bala?
Come and help us make this one.

MAN 1 *doesn't respond.*

MAN 5: I thought this was meant to be a men's group.
MAN 4: I thought we'd just sit around and talk.
MAN 2: You mob always talking. Someone needs to put you to work.
CHORUS (MAN 3, 4, 5): Yeah, good job!
MAN 5: What is this place?

MAN 2: Cook Haus. It's a place where we can gather.

MAN 4: And talk.

MAN 5: Talk shit.

MAN 2: Talk straight … and talk shit.

MAN 3: Easier said than done.

MAN 4: I hear you brother.

MAN 2: The sooner we get these beams on, the sooner I can cook you fellas my special homemade sausages.

MAN 3: Too good.

MAN 2: Oh yeah, this is old school Italian style—with a twist.

MAN 4: Okay …

MAN 2: I've got the usual—pork, beef, chicken, and then I've got a twist—some kangaroo, goanna, emu …

MAN 5: Emu?! I can't eat that! That's my totem.

MAN 2: I hear you—don't worry my brothers, I've got all your totem dietary requirements covered—turtle, dugong and …

He hesitates.

… possum …

CHORUS: Ohhhhhh …

MAN 4: That's disgusting.

MAN 2: It's still in the experimental phase …

MAN 2: C'mon you fellas, this Cook Haus isn't gonna build itself.

The MEN *work to place the beams on the posts. As they do this* MAN 2 *notices* MAN 1 *deep in his thoughts.*

MAN 2: Which way? You are quiet. What troubles you, brother?

MAN 1: Nothing e' right.

MAN 2: There is no shame job here, bala.

MAN 5: What's going on? Whose shame?

MAN 4: Which way?

MAN 2: No-one.

MAN 1: I'm trying to write this letter to my son.

MAN 5: About what?

MAN 2: None of our business. Get back to work!

MAN 4: Is it personal?

MAN 3: It's his business.

MAN 2: Leave him be. If he wants to yarn, he'll yarn.

The MEN *look at* MAN 1, *awaiting his answer ...*

MAN 1: I was just thinking about my son—when he was nine, he tried to take my hand as he always did, and I said, you're too old to hold my hand in public.

I wish I never said it.

MAN 2: I bet at the time you felt it was natural, that when a son reaches a certain age …

MAN 3: A father will feel awkward about demonstrating his affection for him.

MAN 1: I thought this was how a father helped a son to become a man.

MAN 2: But what is it to be a man?

MAN 4: What do you mean?

MAN 2: What shapes how we behave as men, as fathers?

MAN 1: I don't know what to write?

MAN 4: Tell him where he was conceived.

MAN 2: Stop it!

MAN 5: Can't be.

MAN 1: You fellas aren't helping.

MAN 3: Your father must've been over the moon when you told him that you were going to be a dad.

MAN 1: Nah—he just shook his head and told me I was stupid. I didn't fight him. I never did. I just walked away and got on with my stupid life.

MAN 2: That's tough, brother.

MAN 1: I didn't care. I was infatuated with this woman. I'd found the most luscious Garden of Eden.

MAN 4: Ere, look out!

MAN 1: There was only one other direction I wanted to go. I wanted to start a family.

The MEN *have gotten interested in this story as it has grown. They're doing less work now on the Cook Haus and tuning in to this yarn.*

MAN 2: Write about that.

MAN 4: How did you meet her?

MAN 1: I was in Darwin and met her only days after she arrived from Broome.

MAN 5: Ahh, too quick, this crocodile.

MAN 1: We moved in together with her Aunty.

MAN 4: She single?

MAN 2: Ere, knock it off!

MAN 1: We eventually ended up in a tiny caravan. Our daughter's cot took up half the space; it had leaks, infestations and all—but we thought we'd moved into a castle.

MAN 2: Solid!

MAN 1: Life was good. I was working on the wharf and before and after work I'd go fishing. The barramundi inhaling lures in the steamy wet.

MAN 4: Stop it, you're making me hungry.

MAN 1: We didn't have much money back then, so it helped a lot.

He thinks for a moment.

It makes me laugh when I think of my boy as a toddler, watching me getting ready to go to work. He'd hover around me like a little puppy. He'd watch me with those big eyes and ask me, 'Are you going fishing, Dad?' He thought fishing was my work.

MAN 2: How many picanni you got?

MAN 1: Three with her and two with my missus now.

MAN 5: What happened with your ex?

MAN 1: I was twenty-three, with three kids.

I loved being a father, but I wasn't a great husband.

Entering memory sequence.

My boy was four years old, standing between his mother and me when we had our final argument. He was crying, confused and frightened.

We were probably arguing over nothing.

In the heat of the moment, I told her to go back to Broome where she'd come from. The next morning, she was gone, and our three kids were gone.

When I came home from the night shift, the heavy silence filled the house. Toys lay on the floor like corpses. My footsteps echoed between the walls. At night I'd reach across the bed, feeling for her warmth, only to touch the cold sheets.

I lay still in the silence.

What have I done? I've lost my family.

Snap back to the naturalistic world.

MAN 2: Have you spoken to your son about breaking up with his mother?

MAN 1: Nah … nah … and I don't want him to take on that pain, it's not his fault.

MAN 2: But if you don't talk to him, how's he gonna learn in his own relationships?

MAN 2 *walks away to the Cook Haus—leaving* MAN 1 *alone.*

SCENE 2: DREAMS OF MY CHILDHOOD

MAN 4: I didn't have a lot of time with my father—my mum and dad broke up when I was twelve months old. So, my goal as a child was to fix what I felt was broken about my own childhood and be there twenty-four-seven with my kids.

MAN 4 *stands up and starts marking out a handball court. He holds up a ball.*

MAN 4: Who's playing?

MAN 5: Yeah, alright then?

MAN 3: I'll have a go.

MAN 5: I haven't played this in years.

MAN 4: Being a musician working at night, I used to do the school drop-offs. Some parents would drop their kids, then drive to work. But not me …

The MEN *are playing handball. There are some trick shots. The game continues ...*

I started playing handball with my son and all his mates before school. For most kids, it wouldn't be cool to have—your dad—playing handball with you and your friends, but he accepted me. I played like I did back at school and called out all the kids who thought it was okay to cheat!

[*To* MAN 5] Oi! That was out!

The game disbands; the MEN *are puffed.*

MAN 4 *begins noodling on guitar and continues through to a song—'Some Days' by Troy Cassar-Daley.*

MAN 4: When I met his mother, I knew she was the one from the minute I spoke to her. She was gorgeous and smart, and we made each other laugh. When we first got together, I was taken back to the dreams from my childhood of being a father one day. But I also realised I wanted to be a good husband too.

Growing up with my mum, who was a single parent, I always had a huge admiration for strong women. I was surrounded by them—because my aunties were strong as well.

MAN 3: True that, brother.

The other MEN *nod in agreement.*

MAN 4: When my son came into this world, I turned into a child again. I held him and thought, I get to be a father now and be responsible for a little human life. I wanted to always be there, to see it through.

MAN 1: You still with your wife?

MAN 4: Yeah.

MAN 1: How old's your son?

MAN 4: He's twenty-two, living with his girlfriend, making his own way in this world.

MAN 1: You broke the cycle.

MAN 4: Yeah, but it hasn't always been easy either with me and his mother. Sometimes we fight over little things or big things. But I think we've got to where we have today by having respect for each other.

MAN 1: Well, that's it hey, and if someone says they've gotten through life without a bump, they're kidding themselves.

MAN 4 *sings 'Some Days' by Troy Cassar-Daley.*

SCENE 3: I THINK OF YOU, MY SONS

The thrum begins.

The MEN *lay woven mats around the space, creating an island. The tide begins to rise throughout the scene.*

MAN 2: I thank God for blessing me with four strong young warriors, my sons. I think of the sacred place where I feel most at peace, the burial ground where my sixth-generation grandfather rests. I named my eldest son after him. I call this place 'laig' or home. May this sacred place always be their home too.

Coconut palms surround this area.
We eat the fruit hanging from the native trees here.
We sit under the shade of the coconut trees,
listening to the wind as it whistles through the leaves.

MAN 1: I can see crystal blue water.

MAN 3: Shells are in abundance.

MAN 2: When the water hits the beach mark, you can see little pippi shells.

MAN 5: They dance as the waves come in and out.

MAN 1: As the tide changes, they go back into the sand.

MAN 4: I listen to the ocean; it washes and cleanses my mind.

CHORUS: I think of you, my sons.

MAN 2: Butterflies and dragonflies fly around me. My ancestors are with me. I think about when I was a young boy.

CHORUS: It was happiness.

MAN 2: Most of our days were spent down in the water with our cousins. My grandparents would call us turtles because as soon as we woke up, we followed the tide to swim.

We enter a memory space.

MAN 4: As we grew older …

MAN 3: … we turned into goannas.

MAN 5: As goannas, we are taught how to collect turtle eggs.

MAN 4: We are taught how to walk out onto the reef to collect fish.

MAN 2: We sit with our wadhuwam.

CHORUS: Uncles.

MAN 2: They teach us how to make rope and how to splice it.

MAN 1: They teach us how to cut the cassava and replant the stems.

MAN 2: We go diving from the dinghies

MAN 3: Observing our uncles who hunt for dugong and turtle.

MAN 4: When we catch our first fish with a spear, we have a ceremony.

MAN 3: A first catch—means a big feast.

MAN 5: Our matriarch or patriarch has the first bite of the first catch.

MAN 2: My sons, you have experienced these rites of passage.

CHORUS: You are turning into goannas.

MAN 2: My sons, when you see a flock of birds flying as an arrowhead in the sky, you will see the leader at the front; that leader is called

Yathai kuik. Where that bird turns, the flock follows. If that bird goes in the wrong direction, he has an impact on the flock.

As my eldest son, you are the first in line. One day you will be the Yathai kuik. You will be the bird that flies directly behind me in that arrowhead. If anything happens to me, you will replace me as the Yathai kuik and you will be guided by your wadhuwam.

MAN 4: My sons,

MAN 3: You are your brother's bones.

MAN 3: You are your brother's spine.

MAN 1: You are your brother's ribs, his flesh …

MAN 4: His eyes and his ears.

MAN 3: You are his shadow.

MAN 2: You three sons will support your brother.

MAN 1: We are seafaring people.

MAN 3: We are saltwater people.

MAN 2: We must look after our island, the way it has looked after us. The bosom of this land is our mother, and the water surrounding it is our father.

ALL: We have to protect them.

MAN 2: We see the seas wash our island home away.

We are picking up our ancestors' bones as if they are shells, due to the rising seas swallowing our burial grounds.

I am fighting for your future. I am fighting for you to reside in your home.

CHORUS: *Thrumm, thrumm the warup humms*
Yupla com, yupla com
Thrumm, thrumm the warup humms
Yupla com, yupla com
Thrumm, thrumm the warup humms
Yupla com, yupla com
Thrumm, thrumm the warup humms
Yupla com, yupla com

SCENE 4: SCARS OF SURVIVAL

MAN 3: Bumaldhaany Babiin.

Bumaldhaany Babiin.

Each night, I drive past the hospital.

My father is in the neurology ward, he's lost his speech and his movement. He's taken a heavy fall. He's eighty years old and there's no guarantee he will come back from this.

I wind down my window and yell these words.

Bumaldhaany Babiin.

The Bumaldhaany are our warriors. My father is my Babiin. Because of COVID restrictions I can't see him, but I know that somewhere in that hospital he can hear me.

Bumaldhaany Babiin.

Our language will find him, and he will fight because that's what Wiradjuri warriors do: we fight.

He's got scars all over his body:

scars of survival.

Scars from the boxing tents.

Scars from the sawmills.

Scars from the coppers.

Then there are ones we don't see.

Scars that he keeps hidden.

Scars of the soul that don't heal.

He is scarred from Australia.

And there have been times he has been angry.

Other times, Dad was just sad.

I see that deep well of pain, the sadness behind your eyes. They are black eyes, dark pools of history. So much history, so much anger, so much hurt. And all we have left is us. Just us, holding ourselves against the world.

MAN 1 *(silhouette of old man) is using clapsticks, creating a soundscape of dark history, anger and hurt—echoing the dialogue of* MAN 3.

My boys never got to see that. I'm glad they have my memories. And I'm glad they don't have my dad's memories.

MAN 3 *walks over to the silhouette of old man—he now sits down on a chair.*

My boys have only seen a softer side of him. Isn't he beautiful? By the time my boys came along, he didn't need muscles anymore. He didn't have to shape up to the world, he had survived, and he'd found a way to speak back. His way. His words. Our words.

CHORUS: Bumaldhaany Babiin.

MAN 3: He had been sick before and we almost lost him.

The magpies came.

Garru.

Dad saw them in a dream. We were on the front lawn of his house, and we were talking.

The Garru were Dad's father and grandfather.

Wirraye baangaal birra yunaghee.

It's not your time.

Mathu malthan boonmali.

There's more for you to do.

You've given my boys the most wonderful gift. You've given them our language. Because of you, Wiradjuri is protected and preserved forever.

Bumaldhaany Babiin.

I know we won't have you forever. And I'm scared. I am scared because I'm not ready. I am scared because I'm not man enough yet to live without you in this world. I need you to fight just a bit longer to give me time to grow.

The garru (magpies) that have come—walk away—leaving Pop. He will live on and continue his journey in this world.

SCENE 5: SHORTS AND THONGS

The past. We step into a Beat poet-esque road trip with words projected and passing by the father as he recounts how he wrote every memory he could, trying to hold onto moments with the words.

MAN 5: I once tried to write down every memory I could in case it all went bad. So that my son and daughter would one day know me well, walk with me if all went bad.

I wrote my memories as the plump night hours elongated into the skinny, patchy grey of morning, like the leopard-slugs that crawled over our kitchen windowsill back then.

I remember my favourite great-uncle was on FaceTime from his deathbed. He's propped up on pillows with his favourite beer clutched in his hand, wheezing and semi-conscious, asking me when I was coming home.

If he didn't ask … I wouldn't have gone.

I cursed him and loved him a lot on that seventeen-hour run home, my eyes blurring out of focus and shifting sharply back so often I feared I'd drift off the motorway and be greeting Uncle at the next place when he got in.

I drove as fast as I could, collecting my dad on the way.

Son, I wish you could have made the trip with me.

Me and Pop rolled into Port Macquarie getting on midnight.

It wasn't just the dark that made it hard to find our way, the town had changed.

MAN 2: The roads and streets had changed.

MAN 5: It wasn't just me either.

MAN 2: I was lost too.

MAN 5: I was hoping all the while that Uncle was still holding on.

MAN 2: We were close …

MAN 5: Sooo close …

MAN 2: But then …

MAN 5: … we had taken a wayward right turn down a dark, deserted street in an industrial zone.

MAN 2 *and* 3: Gunjibals (police).

MAN 5: An unmarked cop car follows us …

MAN 2: … and flashes its lights.

MAN 5: I climbed out from behind the wheel, phone screen glowing in full view, your Pop swearing and thinking the worst was about to unfold.

MAN 2: Stop harassing us, you bloody bastards!

MAN 5: Dad! Sorry, you see, it's my uncle—he's on his deathbed. We're lost and the map says we're close, like five hundred and ten metres close.

We got off.

MAN 2 *and* 3: This time.

MAN 5: Your Pop led the way.

MAN 2: In the dark, the street numbers were not clear …

MAN 5: But finally, after seventeen hours of driving, your Pop guided me into the driveway. I cut the engine after parking on the front lawn.

Your Pop opened the door …

MAN 2: And we was walking down the hallway …

MAN 5: When I spotted photos on the wall … wait a minute … whose??

MAN 4: It's the wrong house!

MAN 5: [*thinking of son*] Son, it made me think of you and how much I always want time to stand still. You, always in my arms and me, always strong enough to carry you as far as needed.

But … time doesn't stand still …

… and facing a startled stranger …

MAN 2: And his terrified wife …

MAN 4 *screams.*

MAN 5: … I felt the moving of time was fortuitous. And like time, everything happened so quickly.

MAN 2: No doubt the gunjies were called …

MAN 3: [*over the radio*] Home invasion under progress in your area.

MAN 1: Two perps, both male; the first described as grey, possibly blind in one eye, wearing shorts and thongs.

MAN 3: The second also grey, heavily bearded, reeking of highway coffee; also wearing shorts and thongs.

MAN 2: We piled into the car … which fortunately fired up first go.

MAN 5: Son, at this point I want you to know that you have helped me get through some pretty tough times.

I was up the mountain looking over our Country, the way north, the way south, right along the coast.

It was the day before Invasion Day.

I was having a quiet, reflective moment, cursing all the Flaggies that had infested our lands below.

Then the call came.

Uncle had passed away while I was up the hill. Dylan's 'Dead Man' jumped back into the car's speakers, while the plains that Uncle had asked to be buried on, slipped by, silently on my right.

SCENE 6: THE GREATEST LOVE STORY EVER TOLD

MAN 1 *is looking at the bicycle. He pops it upside down and spins the wheel—it has a card in the wheel and makes an engine sound—before placing the bike back on the ground.* MAN 2 *looks at the bike and picks off a star from it. Memories flood back.*

Enter memory space.

MAN 4 *enters.*

MAN 4: Son, can I have smoke?

MAN 2: I can't, Dad.

MAN 4: Ask the nurse if I can have a smoke?

MAN 2: [*to himself*] I knew you smoked all your life, but it never entered my mind that it might be killing you.

MAN 4: What did she say? Did she say I can have a smoke?

MAN 2: No Dad, she said you're on oxygen and it's too dangerous.

MAN 4: Did she say that? You sure?

MAN 2 *pulls a star (Malvern Star) out of the box. It reminds him of a story.*

MAN 2: Here's the star you followed across the country—the Malvern Star. I think the Malvern Star Australian bike adventure was your most legendary endeavour. I sometimes think of you back in 1926 when you were approached by a small bike shop owner in Melbourne.

A scene plays out with CHORUS *and with* MAN 2 *taking a narrator type of role, recollecting the memory from his father's memoirs.*

MAN 5 *starts blowing up a balloon.*

SIR BRUCE SMALL/MAN 1: I want to show you something.

He walks over with a young DAD. *A blanket draped over something.*

DAD *looks at* SIR BRUCE SMALL, *before ...*

Go on, unveil it.

DAD *removes the blanket, revealing a shiny Malvern Star bicycle.*

I'm calling it the Malvern Star.

MAN 4: The Melbourne Star.

MAN 1: No no, the Malvern Star.

MAN 4: Yeah, that's what I said—Melbourne Star.

MAN 1: Malvern Star … ah, forget it. Point is, I want you to promote it for me.

MAN 4: How?

SIR BRUCE SMALL/MAN 1: I want you to ride it around Australia. Catch is, you need to do it in less than seven months and twenty-eight days.

MAN 4: Why's that?

SIR BRUCE SMALL/MAN 1: It's the Australian record and I want you to break it.

Looks at the bicycle.

On this.

And you better take a riding partner,
who knows what the hell is in the outback.

MAN 2: Yeehaw!

So, you hit the road with your mate.

Two MEN *are riding Malvern Star bicycles. Another* ACTOR *is rotating a background scenery as if riding. The guys are riding but the background scenery isn't moving. Then one of them squeezes his horn on his bike, alerting the* ACTOR*—who then starts rotating the background scenery.*

MAN 4: We ride the east coast to Brisbane, then west to Mount Isa. From there, onwards west and into the Northern Territory and then almost at Katherine.

MAN 1 *pops balloon: BANG!*

What the hell was that?

MAN 3: I shot myself.

MAN 4: Where the hell did you get that gun from?

MAN 3: In my trousers.

MAN 4: Friggin' bastard.

MAN 3: I was afraid … you know … of the Aboriginal people …
I heard they're cannibals.

MAN 2: What a ride the last few hundred kilometres must have been for you.

DAD *and* DAD'S FRIEND *continue riding. Though only now* DAD'S FRIEND *is riding with one leg straight out and pedalling only with the other leg.*

When you made it to Darwin, you were so exhausted and got sunstroke so bad you went to hospital in a coma. When you came to, you opened your eyes.

And this is how you tell it …

MAN 4: Standing by my bed was an angel.

A silhouette of an angel is illuminated. The CHORUS *vocalise.*

MAN 2: You thought you'd died and gone to heaven, and the angels were …

MAN 4: Aboriginal?

MAN 2: Dad, I think yours and Mum's is the greatest love story ever told.

It would have been hard back then … you know, you being a white man who loved an Aboriginal woman.

You both came from completely different worlds.

His attention turns to his dad. Speaking directly to his spirit.

Dad, I never told you how much I admire you. I regret I never told you how much I love you while you were alive.

MAN 4 *strums 'Windradyne' by Troy Cassar-Daley on the guitar.*

SCENE 7: BE HONEST, BROTHER

Cook Haus. The MEN *clear the space.*

MAN 1: I'm finding this really hard, there is so much to these letters we're writing to our sons and fathers.

MAN 2: There is such a great responsibility to be a father, to step up to that role to guide one's children, to be a pillar of strength in the family and community.

MAN 4: And just be honest brother, and your words will take the clay material of the past—and shape them into a gift for the future.

MAN 4 *sings 'Windradyne' by Troy Cassar-Daley on the guitar. The* MEN *change costume. Projection—Colonial labels begin to invade the space again.*

MAN 2: Hey fellas, I'm gonna put on some sausages and burgers soon. Anyone here a vegetarian?

The MEN *laugh.*

What you gotta ask these days.

MAN 5: What blakfullas are vegetarian?

MAN 4: [*slightly awkward*] I am.

MAN 5: Aye, true, bro. That's deadly.

MAN 1: Too good, bro.

MAN 4: Better for the digestion, you know.

MAN 2: I got some vege burgers here too.

MAN 4: Thanks, bala.

MAN 2: Anyone else wanna try a vege burger?

CHORUS: Na ee right bro.

MAN 2: Everyone okay with onions?

CHORUS: All good.

MAN 2: Who wants to give me a hand with the salad?

Pause.

MAN 5: Yeah bro, pass me that baby cos, I'll chop him up.

ACT II—LETTERS OF LOSS

SCENE 8: PERHAPS IN HEAVEN

A large projection of a Blak Douglas artwork is projected, creating an animated landscape of his imagination in which this scene plays out. The image is still, except for animated clouds that slowly drift.

MAN 1: There was an unwritten law in the western suburbs of Sydney where I was raised. To be seen to hug your father at school drop-off demonstrated gayness.

MAN 1 *goes to hug* FATHER/MAN 2.

MAN 3: God forbid, honey!

MAN 1: And to so much as kiss your dad on the cheek—

MAN 1 *goes to kiss* FATHER/MAN 2.

CHORUS: No way!

MAN 3: Holding back affection was like damming a river. It was emotional torture, a ridiculous homophobia.

MAN 1: I'm an artist, I make a living with my paints and canvas. I fight racism through creative expression. My dad made a living through labouring. He fought against racism with his fists and brawn.

He was born in Thubbagah (Dubbo), around the time of the Second World War—an era when some Blakfullas were still being neck-shackled and chained to trees.

I was born and raised in the suburbs of the big city, yet in my lifetime, the neck shackles were swapped for handcuffs.

In Dad's school photos, he's the only identifiable Koori amongst a dozen white kids.

His dark brown skin and piercing blue eyes made him stand out like a cheetah in a chook pen. They said

... you had the speed of a cheetah too.

He told me he was popular, until one day a kid used the term ...

CHORUS: Boong!

MAN 1: It must have been hard for him.

MAN 2: Wanna have a go, yer black bastard?

MAN 1: Into his adulthood, the racism continued.

MAN 5: Wanna have a go, yer black bastard?

MAN 1: Each time he entered a pub, the shenanigans would begin.

MAN 3: Wanna have a go, yer black bastard?

MAN 1: … and on the footy field.

CHORUS: Wanna have a go, yer black bastard?

Sound of 'DING DING'. A cheer and for a fleeting moment we're ringside at a boxing match.

FIGHT COMMENTATOR/MAN 3: And so, the Blak man is against the ropes once again. Only way for him is to fight.

FIGHT COMMENTATOR/MAN 2: He better be good with his fists.

FIGHT COMMENTATOR/MAN 3: It's the end of the week, and you know what that means.

FIGHT COMMENTATOR/MAN 2: It's beeeeeeeerrr o'clock.

FIGHT COMMENTATOR/MAN 3: And shit's about to hit the fan.

FIGHT COMMENTATOR/MAN 2: Especially when he has eyes for a young barmaid.

FIGHT COMMENTATOR/MAN 3: Because the problem is …

MAN 2 *and* 3: She's white.

Sound: 'DING DING'.

FIGHT COMMENTATOR/MAN 2: It's a knockout!

MAN 1: The barmaid you fought for became my mum.

I remember this saying with affection, now that you're gone.

'It's not often I am right, but I am never wrong.'

MAN 1: I remember that saying.

I'd hastily got a mate to drive all the way up to Cessnock to lay down ten grand on a used V-8 Commodore station wagon.

CHORUS: Vroom, Vroom, Vroom.

MAN 1: Dad!

MAN 2: He said.

MAN 1: It'll be perfect for my school art-show tours!

MAN 3: Yeah, right—

MAN 1: Was your reply, with your unrivalled tone of inflection.

CHORUS: Vroom, Vroom, Vroom

MAN 1: There was no way I was going to leave Cessnock without that …

CHORUS: … Metallic green machine … Vroom.

MAN 1: I haggled …

MAN 3: … At least enough to pay for fuel to get there.

MAN 1: A test drive around the block and I was / sold!

CHORUS: / Sold!! Vroom, Vroom, Vroom.

MAN 1: What a dream this was to drive this thing back to Penrith.

MAN 1 *mimes driving the car back to Penrith.*

MAN 2: CD player!

MAN 3: Tape deck!

MAN 5: Six-speed manual.

CHORUS: Vroom, Vroom, Vroom.

MAN 2: Five-point-seven litres and cruise control.

MAN 1: After only ten Ks, I had already devised modification plans.

MAN 3: Back home.

MAN 5: After spending a hundred and thirty-three bucks at the bowser.

MAN 1: I pulled into the driveway, giving a few unnecessary revs to announce the arrival of the chariot.

CHORUS: Vroom, Vroom, Vroom.

MAN 1: You walked out.

FATHER *walks towards* SON *looking at the Green Machine as the* SON *recalls.*

Adjusting your tracksuit pants like Louis the Fourteenth adjusting his sword.

FATHER *grabs and adjusts his tracksuit pants.*

You began assessing …

FATHER *is ducking and weaving around the vehicle checking the lines, looking for rust. He stops at the front of the vehicle and steps back and puts his hand on his chin.*

… you lowered your scrutinising gaze. Keeping your head at the same altitude, you took several paces back …

CHORUS: She's been in a head-on.

Vroom … Vroom …

Splutters.

MAN 1: Bullshit, Dad.

FATHER *grabs* MAN 1, *leans in, pointing to the left-hand edge of the bonnet, then the front left indicator, pointing out the differences in the gaps.*

CHORUS: Bullshit Dad, bullshit Dad, bullshiiiiittt.

FATHER *backs away, leaving* MAN 1 *on his own.*

MAN 1: The following year, when I had some repairs done the mechanic validated your astute observation.

CHORUS: It's not often I'm right, but I'm never wrong.

MAN 1: I miss you and Mum, Dad.

My heart melted when you became Mum's full-time carer after she had a stroke. The love you demonstrated—the level of care you gave her was deep and constant.

I truly miss you, Dad.

Perhaps in heaven there is no unwritten law against two men showing each other affection. And even if there is, like down here, some laws need to be broken.

SCENE 9: THE TALK

MAN 3: I remember the day I made the decision to have the 'the talk' talk with my son.

MAN 4: Oh, 'the talk'.

MAN 3: I had to tell him sooner or later. I was extremely nervous. And unsure whether I was doing the right thing.

MAN 1: Time and tide waits for no-one, brother.

Lights change. We enter memory space.

MAN 3: Son, you wanna go to the park? It's a lovely day, blue skies—a great day to be out kicking the footy.

Son—I … I … You are … You and your sister have amazing sporting skills. So, so talented. It's safe to say you didn't inherit the sporty gene from me.

MAN 3 *gives a forced laugh.*

Do you remember when you were learning to ride your bike? The bike was so big, and you were sooo small, but you never gave up. Eventually you found your balance and rode away with confidence and a huge smile I will never forget.

You display the courage and resilience I sometimes forget to have.
Thank you for reminding me, son.
[*To son*] I'm gay.
[*To son*] I am gay.

Returns from memory space to Cook Haus space.

[*To other* MEN] I *am* gay.

Pause.

[*Speaking to the* MEN] He doesn't even flinch. He just carries on being my son. Clearly, it was harder for me to tell him I am gay than it was for him to know that I am.

The MEN *enjoy a laugh.*

I had decided to be true to myself. To no longer deny my sexuality. To accept that I was gay, no longer hiding who I was. Being true to myself healed me.

CHORUS: Good on ya coordah/brother/bala/ngoonie/tidda [*etc.*]

MAN 3: Being gay does not define me. I am still a proud dad—full of love and gratitude for the miracle and blessing of my son and my daughter. I want them to know that the most important thing is to be true to yourself.

As a result of the courage and strength to speak so personally, MAN 3 *has given the* MEN *permission to do the same.*

SCENE 10: KEEP LOVING MATE

Sound of a whistle being blown, and crowd cheering on commentary of a footy game ...

MAN 5: I was lucky enough to play sport as my job for years—first as an NRL player for the mighty South Sydney Rabbitohs.

The MEN *sing the Rabbitohs theme song.*

CHORUS: Glory, glory to South Sydney.

MAN 5: My sporting career was a blessing. But my greatest achievement was being a dad to five of the best kids any parent could wish for.
When I first laid eyes on my oldest boy, I thought, how on earth could I have played a part in producing someone so beautiful?

MAN 1: With a mug like that.

MAN 3: Must've got his looks from his mother.
MAN 5: I was also a professional boxer.
My long son—that's what I called him because of his long arms and legs.

A boxing bell rings.

COMMENTATOR/MAN 4: Here we are, ladies and gentlemen—it's on!
He's backing up now—stalking him—measuring—
Here it comes—
Cracks him under the chin—
Down he goes! Dropped like a stone!
And he's not getting up—
No way he's getting up!
That's it—that's all she wrote!
MAN 5: Everyone thought I was successful.
Let's hear it for the champ!
My shout!
Here you go brother, skull this one.
C'mon, let's celebrate!
I partied and drank alcohol.
But I was battling the enemy within.
The alcohol—a band-aid on my feelings.

He sings the Rabbitohs theme song.

Chant continues to fade into the background.

I lost my family—my long son was only five years old.
The band-aid wasn't working.
I needed to get sober.
But once I took the alcohol out of my system,
the noise became louder in my head.

He's back in the ring; this time his mind is his opponent—he's copping the punches.

The MEN *stand as pillars of the boxing ring—three of them with their back toward him, heads bowed.*

And now the words hit his body like actual punches. Each line lands physically. The commentary is distorted, sounds loop or glitch ...

COMMENTATOR: [*distorted*] He's backing up now … stalking him—measuring—
Here it comes—Cracks him under the chin—Down he goes!
And he's not getting up—
No way he's getting up!

He drops to his knees.

The three MEN *walk slowly away, leaving him on his own.*

MAN 5: But I did, eventually.
Son … I'm sorry.
I didn't think.
I didn't see what it was doing to you.
Or your sister. Or your mum.
I was selfish.
I'm sorry.

MAN 2 *breaks the dreamscape.*

Connecting to Country has been healing for me. I had to be honest, with myself, with everyone around me.

Healing is a continual journey.

MAN 2: If your son was here now, what would you say to him?

MAN 5: Son, don't ever think it is shameful to show your vulnerability. There is enormous strength in being vulnerable. And always love and look after your mum and respect all women.

You came from a mother and will return to Mother Earth.

And finally—love—love is the key to growth in anyone's heart. Keep loving, mate. Love with everything you have. The world needs less hate, and more love.

SCENE 11: SOMEHOW THE SUN WAS OFF-CENTRE

MAN 3 *washes his father's feet (*MAN 2 / DAD*).*

MAN 1: The last time I spoke to my dad it was late at night. The conversation was brief, it had to be. He could barely breathe …

MAN 2/DAD: 'I'm not in pain, son, I'm just … it's frustrating,

I want to see my grandchildren. They need to see their Pop one last time.'

MAN 1: We couldn't get to him in Echuca until Wednesday.

MAN 2/DAD: 'Wednesdee?'

I need to say it to them, and they need to hear it from me.

MAN 1: He was gone early the next morning. The sky was so red, sailor's warning.

Continues washing his father's body.

I'll always remember the time he refused to pay to get into the local footy game. His story even made it into the *Euroa Gazette*. The High Court had just handed down the Mabo decision. And white people thought that Blak people like us were coming to take their land … I wonder what that feels like. But Dad never lost his sense of humour.

Memory space—we're at the footy oval.

MAN 2/DAD: Five bucks! What are you talking about?

MAN 3: It's five bucks to enter if you want to see Euroa versus Mooroopna!

MAN 2/DAD: Don't you know who I am?

MAN 3: Um, no, sir.

MAN 2/DAD: I'm Billy James.

MAN 3: Yes … and?

MAN 2/DAD: And … I'm Aboriginal, son.

MAN 3: Oh, that's wonderful.

MAN 2/DAD: Yes. Yes, it is. And do you see that football oval behind you?

MAN 3 *turns to look.*

MAN 2/DAD: That's my land. Now under the new Native Title laws, i.e. Mabo versus the State of Queensland 1992, I'm permitted to have access to my land.

MAN 3: Your land? The footy field?

MAN 2/DAD: Yes. Sacred land! Now—you don't think I should have to pay to have access to my sacred land—do you?

MAN 3: Ah, well, um … I need to ask my manager.

MAN 1: In the newspaper article it says—'The resultant conversation can't be recorded in your family newspaper. To cut a long story short, Billy finally paid.'

MAN 2/DAD: Under sufferance!

MAN 1: When I came back to spend time with him, he was the last Blakfulla in town. He'd got his final tattoo by then, a small Koori flag across his chest. Somehow the sun was off centre, probably because his heart was so big that it had its own centre of gravity.

Pause.

At home in your last years, you would sit staring across the corrugated-iron rooftop of the neighbour's home, watching the tall ghost gum changing colour and form in the afternoon light.

It was mesmerising, the last of its ghostly glow disappearing at dusk.

Dad, I wonder how many of your thoughts, feelings and regrets are caught in that majestic tree's foliage. If I think of you now Dad, it is that tree by the creek.

SCENE 12: A SINGLE IMAGE

The MEN *come up and stand around* MAN 4 *in a half-circle, embrace arm in arm.*

MAN 4: I'm lying on the couch with my son on my chest,

The MEN *take deep breaths together.*

I'm watching his little mannerisms while he sleeps.

The moment is perfect.

The phone rings.

My sister calls—out of the blue.

Mum's gone.

The MEN *take a long exhale.*

MAN 4 *presses his hand over his chest, holding his son and his broken heart. A silence.*

And then, a few days later, on telly … ABC *Four Corners*. Don Dale.

Sound of prison doors closing. The MEN *break apart—standing like* PRISON GUARDS. *Two* GUARDS *turn on one—*MAN 3 *who becomes the* PRISONER, *restraining and forcing him to the ground.*

One guard exits—returning with a chair, straitjacket and hood.

The GUARDS *drag the* PRISONER *to the chair roughly, placing a mask and straitjacket on him.*

The PRISONER *(*MAN 3*) writhes, muffled, breaths loud, body fighting, then slumping. The* GUARDS *step back and turn their backs to the audience.*

[*Voice steady but breaking*] I thought of my son.
Profiled for criminal intent …
… because he's Blak.
August fourth—National Children's Day for Aboriginal and Torres Strait Islander people.
A day to celebrate.
Acknowledge our children …
… and their belonging to this Country.
But instead.
A cartoon in *The Australian* newspaper. It says …

Flickering image of cartoon (inverted image).

And then to black as police spotlight shines on MEN. *Guilty!*

Aboriginal men …
CHORUS: [*spotlight*] … are drunks.

The words strike like a punch in the gut.

MAN 4: Aboriginal men …
CHORUS: … don't know their children.

Another punch.

MAN 4: Aboriginal men …
CHORUS: Don't care.

Another punch.

MAN 4: A single image …
Undermining my love—for my children.
A single image …
… belittling my relationship with my parent.
A single image …
… shifting the blame.
CHORUS: [*pondering*] … a single image.

MAN 1: Meanwhile, back at my home, the government enacts the Northern Territory Intervention. And this time, they paint an image of Aboriginal men as …

CHORUS: Molesters …

… doers of evil …

MAN 1: They send in the army, with signs.

Alcohol.

CHORUS: Banned.

MAN 1: Pornography.

CHORUS: Banned.

MAN 1: [*in disbelief*] Most of our men didn't even know what pornography was.

CHORUS: Guilty.

MAN 1: Standing in the supermarket.

Lights lower—and PRISONER *is highlighted. The* MEN *circle around him.*

I can feel all these whitefullas looking at me.

They pull his chair away from him. One ties a strap around him, and they drag him around the stage.

CHORUS: [*whispering*] Molester.

MAN 1: I could see it.

CHORUS: [*whispering*] Bastard.

MAN 1: I could feel it.

CHORUS: [*whispering*] Molester.

MAN 1: What are you staring at!?

The MEN *leave the* PRISONER *lying there on the ground, left for dead.*

MAN 5 *comes over to* PRISONER*—looks at him for a moment. Then punches him, before walking away.*

MAN 3 *bleeds, left for dead.*

SCENE 13: IT SPREAD LIKE WILDFIRE

The sound of sheets of corrugated iron rattling and moaning in the wind, distant creaks, faint clanging—conjuring the memory of the Bungalow.

MAN 3/PRISONER: Blue eyes.
The bastard had blue eyes.

The MEN *help him stand and remove his hood.*

My father was stolen from his mum, when he was five years old.
My father rarely swore—proper gentleman.
But on his deathbed, that's what rose up.
One memory. One face.
The bastard had blue eyes.

A long breath.

The boys were groomed to be stockmen.
The girls to be housekeepers and servants.

CHORUS: Child after child—stolen.

MAN 1: Taken to the Bungalow.

MAN 2: Stolen. Schooled. Enslaved.

MAN 4: Abused.

MAN 5: The pain sunk within.

MAN 1: Sentenced to a life of nightmares.

MAN 2: Only the grog could numb the pain.

Beat.

MAN 3: We have every right to be angry.

MAN 1: We have every cause to be angry.

MAN 3: There's too much anger in this world.

MAN 4: Too many images of hate.
And that's why, brothers, when I looked at my children, I said to myself—I am a proud Aboriginal dad. And my children make me a proud Aboriginal dad. I posted a picture of me with my children.

Projection on screen: '#IndigenousDads'.

MAN 2: #IndigenousDads? That was you, brother?

MAN 4: Yeah, and I wasn't the only one who felt this way.

MAN 3: It spread like wildfire.

MAN 5: Thousands of pictures posted.

MAN 2: Photos of Aboriginal and Torres Strait Islander men and their children.

MAN 3: Aboriginal women and their fathers.

MAN 1: Community activists.

MAN 4: Politicians.

MAN 5: Sporting stars.

MAN 4: I couldn't believe it. Something so good came from something so bad. I said to my son—you see truth-telling allows a person … a people …

ALL: … a Country, to heal.

ACT III—LETTERS OF LOVE

SCENE 14: HEART OF THE COMMUNITY

Fanny Cochrane-Smith recordings from 1899 play, including speaking and singing.

MAN 2: This language is palawa kani, keeping our Elders and our Country close. Like a thread that connects us through every word we speak.

Hold on to this thread, so you never get lost, son.

Great-great-grandma Fanny Smith is one of the reasons why palawa kani exists today.

Echo of Fanny Cochrane-Smith song recording.

These recordings provided the community with the opportunity to revive our language. Even though I only know a handful of words of palawa kani, I have spoken it to my son since he was in the womb.

Ya malangina mina.

MAN 4: Hello, my son.

MAN 2: Nika milaythina palawa,

MAN 4: This is palawa country,

MAN 2: Milaythina mana.

MAN 4: My country.

MAN 2: palawa takara milaythina nara-mapali-ta.

MAN 4: palawa have walked our country forever.

MAN 2: palawa mulaka, palawa kanaplila,

MAN 4: palawa have hunted, sung and danced forever,

MAN 2: palawa krakapaka milaythina nara-mapali-ta.

MAN 4: palawa have died on our country.

MAN 2: Waranta tunapri tunapri palawa.

We palawa have deep knowledge and deep connection.

That recording was her letter to us. So we would never lose the thread. Grandma Smith was the heart of the community. She'd welcome guests with love and always have food for them to share.

Maybe that's why my wife and I decided to start a business called palawa kipli—means palawa food—to follow her thread. We created this business with a focus on Aboriginal food, but we added a modern twist and homage to my wife's Mexican heritage.

Our favourite dish is a Mexican-inspired tortilla infused with wattle seed and topped with bush-tucker ingredients. We call it the Bush-Taco. The single best mix of our cultures, until our son was born.

For our son's first birthday, we dressed him up as the world's first Aboriginal astronaut. It might have seemed silly, but that is our wish for him, to keep his culture close to him. To take the thread of his past and dream it into his future.

MAN 2 *drops 'character', steps forward and introduces himself.*

Each of the actors do the same.

'My name is ...'

'My relationship with my son and/or father is ...'

'My hope for the future is ...'

Photos of the actors and their own children and/or dads are projected.

To our children …

We are the first builders,

MAN 5: craftsmen,

MAN 4: storytellers,

MAN 2: artists.

MAN 3: We are the first fishermen,

MAN 1: hunters,

MAN 4: scientists,

MAN 5: inventors,

MAN 2: explorers,

MAN 3: farmers,

MAN 1: engineers,

ALL: warriors, and healers.

MAN 2: We are not conquerors of each other's lands.

MAN 3: We do not strangle Mother Earth.

MAN 5: We are her protectors.

MAN 1: We are all these things and so much more.

MAN 4: We are a continuum of proud Aboriginal and Torres Strait Islander men—

MAN 1: The fathers of the longest surviving culture on earth.

CHORUS: With the strength of our ancestors.

MAN 2: We pull the oars of truth …

MAN 1: Against the tides of ignorance and toxic masculinity.

CHORUS: With the strength of our ancestors …

MAN 5: Our words, as bright as the stars on a moonless night.

MAN 4: We offer our children.

MAN 3: Shining points of guidance.

CHORUS: We pull the oars of truth …

We are left with the sound of the calm ocean.

MAN 1: Dear Son …

MAN 2: Dear Son.

MAN 3: Dear Son.

MAN 4: Dear Son.

MAN 5: Dear Son.

Their words, continuing the legacy of their ancestors, hold space and time for their families and communities.

THE END